Early
One Morning

Written by Greg Lang
Illustrated by Bettina Guthridge

sundance

Early one morning, Anna got out of bed.
She got dressed.
She put on her hat.
She put on her scarf.
She found her shoes
and put them on, too.

Dad was waiting for her in the kitchen.
"Sshh!" he said. "Don't wake the others."

They went out the front door.
They had something important to do.
"I like being up early," said Anna.
"Me, too," said Dad.

As they walked down the sidewalk, Anna and her dad saw the town waking up.

Someone was taking milk to the shop. Garbage trucks were collecting the trash. The street sweeper was cleaning the road.

7

They saw a boy delivering papers.
They saw a woman walking her dog.
They saw two people jogging.
They saw a man going fishing.
They saw a bird sitting on a wall.

9

But Anna and her dad
walked to the bakery.
They had something important to do.

"That smells good," they said.
"Warm, fresh bread. Mmm. Yum!"

They bought some warm bread and some muffins.
They bought two rolls.

"One for you and one for me," said Dad.

They ate the rolls as they walked home.

14

When they got home, everyone
was still asleep.

They set the table and put the bread
and the muffins on the table.

"Go and wake everyone up, Anna,"
said Dad.

"Everybody! Breakfast is ready!"
Anna called.

"That smells good," Mom said.
"Warm, fresh bread. Mmm. Yum!"

"Good morning, Mom!" said Anna.